MW00593615

At David C Cook, we equip the local church around the corner and around the globe to make disciples. Come see how we are working together—go to **www.davidccook.com**. Thank you!

KNOWING JESUS

DAVID C COOK FAMILY DEVOTIONS

KNOWING JESUS

*52 Devotions to Grow
Your Family's Faith*

DAVID C COOK

transforming lives together

KNOWING JESUS
Published by David C Cook
4050 Lee Vance Drive
Colorado Springs, CO 80918 U.S.A.

Integrity Music Limited, a Division of David C Cook
Eastbourne, East Sussex BN23 6NT, England

The graphic circle C logo is a registered trademark of David C Cook.

LCCN 2018931601
ISBN 978-1-4347-1250-9
eISBN 978-0-8307-7573-6

© 2018 Beers Family Real Estate LLC
Published in association with the literary agency of
Mark Sweeney & Associates, Naples, FL 34113.

The Team: Lindsay Black, Jeff Gerke, Rachael Stevenson, Jane Ann Kenney
Cover Design: Nick Lee
Cover Illustration: Oliver Genoux

Printed in the United States of America
First Edition 2018

1 2 3 4 5 6 7 8 9 10

062818

CONTENTS

NOTE TO PARENTS

You are about to begin a delightful journey with a child, using this book as your road map. Whether you are a parent, grandparent, uncle, aunt, teacher, neighbor, or some other special person with the great privilege of leading children God's way, praise God for you.

This is a devotional book to help children—*and* you—know Jesus better, love Him more deeply, and serve Him more effectively.

The first section in every devotion is a poetry-style passage to read aloud to your child. This is designed to engage your child with the opening Bible verse in a way that lights their imagination and touches their hearts.

The "Grow Your Faith" section is for you to read to yourself, perhaps before you sit down with your child. This section leads you to interact with the passage and some aspect of Jesus in a way that may challenge and inspire you. This could help prepare you if the other parts of the reading give rise to a discussion with your child.

This is followed by a section called "Grow Your Child's Faith." This is also designed to be read aloud to your child. It extends the original thought and brings application in ways he or she can use in real life.

Each devotion concludes with a suggested prayer your child could say to Jesus. If a prayer isn't exactly what the child is thinking or feeling right then, encourage him or her to adjust it so it becomes an authentic expression to God.

It is our prayer that as you and your child learn more about Jesus, you will forge an unforgettable bond in which your hearts and Jesus' heart become knitted together in love.

JESUS IS FOREVER

In the beginning was the Word.
John 1:1

What's the oldest thing you know?

An ancient tree?
The mountains or the sea?
The earth? The moon?
The sun? Outer space?

What could be even older?
Who has been since the beginning?

Jesus.

Grow Your Faith

Although Jesus was born on a specific day in a specific year, just like all humans have ever been, that birthday is not the beginning of Jesus' life. He has existed as God since before time began, and He will still be God after time ends. Jesus is, has always been, and will always be … forever.

Grow Your Child's Faith

Wouldn't it be strange not to have a birthday? Your birthday marks the day you breathed air for the first time and started really being you. Jesus existed long before He was born to Mary. He existed even before time existed! And Jesus doesn't end. He will always keep going into the forever future. You can live with Him forever!

Dear Jesus, thank You that You are forever! That makes it easy to depend on You in every situation. Amen.

JESUS IS THE LIVING WORD

The Word was with God, and the Word was God.
John 1:1

Can a word be alive?

The written Word is the Bible,
what God says.
The Living Word is Jesus,
who God is.

The written Word is approved
by the Living Word
and teaches us about Him.

Grow Your Faith

Through the Bible, we come to know the person of Jesus. Getting to know Him is easier when we have the written Word in our hands. How do you study the Bible? How can you help your child study the Bible too?

Grow Your Child's Faith

Have you ever read a book about someone that was so good you really felt like you knew the person? The Bible tells us about God. Four very special books tell us about Jesus' life. We get to know Jesus in our hearts, but we also come to know Him by reading about Him in the Bible.

Dear Jesus, I'm glad I can read all about You so I can know who You are, how You work, and how You love! Amen.

JESUS IS CREATOR OF EVERYTHING

Through him all things were made; without him
nothing was made that has been made.

John 1:3

Jesus worked with
God the Father and the Holy Spirit
to create everything there is.

Honeybees and elephants, wildflowers and clouds,
rainbows and robins, and you and I
all exist because of Jesus!

Jesus must be God
to make all these amazing things!

Grow Your Faith

Sometimes we struggle to believe Jesus really knows us and cares
about the things that concern us. But the One who cares for the
smallest cell and the largest galaxy without breaking a sweat will
certainly pay attention to us—the only creatures made in the
image of God.

Grow Your Child's Faith

We can create things in our imaginations, but we have to use materials that already exist, like paper, crayons, a computer, or paint, to make things. Not Jesus! Everything that exists is here because Jesus made it. Even more amazing: Jesus created it all *from nothing.*

Dear Jesus, You've made so many amazing things. Please make me more creative like You. Amen.

4

JESUS IS THE SOURCE OF ALL LIFE

In him was life.
John 1:4

There are two kinds of life.
One is here on earth.
The other is with Jesus in heaven.

Life on earth will end one day.
Life in heaven will never end.
Jesus is the maker of both kinds of life.

Grow Your Faith

With Jesus, life began. Without Jesus, life ends. With Jesus, life never ends. Our mortal lives are our opportunities to choose eternal life with Jesus. Once we have chosen Jesus, our job is to make sure others have the opportunity to choose Jesus. Who needs you to tell them about that choice? This life is the only chance they'll get to make it.

Grow Your Child's Faith

What is your favorite animal? What is your favorite plant? Who is your favorite person? There is One person who dreamed up and made every one of those living things—even the angels! Can you say His name?

Dear Jesus, thank You for making all life, from my best friend to my favorite sea creature. Thank You for making it possible for me to live with You forever! Amen.

JESUS IS THE SOURCE OF ALL LIGHT

His life brought light to everyone.
John 1:4 NLT

Without light from the sun,
plants get sick and die.
Without light from God's Son,
people get sick too.

Jesus is the Light of the World.
He is the hope shining in the darkness.
Like a candle in the dark.
Like a lighthouse in a storm.

Grow Your Faith

Jesus said we are the light of the world (Matt. 5:14)—as Christ-followers, our good deeds show that God is worthy of praise. Without Christ, we would be "without hope and without God in the world" (Eph. 2:12). What a horrific state of being! How are you shining the light that is in you?

Grow Your Child's Faith

Your friends and family who don't have Jesus in their hearts are like people stumbling through a forest without a light. They don't know where they are, where they are going, or the dangers that may be right in front of them. Jesus is the Light of the World! How can you help someone you love find Him?

Dear Jesus, You shine like the brightest searchlight on the darkest night. You show us the way to heaven. Please shine through me so others can find You. Amen.

JESUS HELPS US BECOME GOD'S CHILDREN

To all who did receive him, to those who believed in his
name, he gave the right to become children of God.
John 1:12

Another name for Christian
is child of God.

God wants each person to be
His child,
but He doesn't force anyone
to call Him "Father."

No one is God's child
until he or she chooses
to believe in Jesus and follow Him—
the Son of God.

Grow Your Faith

Perhaps you know a family that has lovingly adopted a child. In that home, no distinction is made between the adopted child and the biological child. Enveloping the adopted child in their love is natural and joyful. When God adopts us as children, we become brothers and sisters of Jesus Himself, just like we had always belonged in the family.

Grow Your Child's Faith

How do your parents take care of you? They make sure you are safe, stay healthy, and also get to have some fun. That's what it's like to be God's child too! Except God is the one taking care of you—and Jesus is your big brother!

Dear Jesus, I love the thought that You're my big brother. What big-brother stuff do You want to teach me? Amen.

JESUS IS GOD AND MAN

The Word became a human being and lived here with us.
John 1:14 CEV

God the Son
was born as a baby,
grew up as a boy,
and became a man.

Jesus came to earth
and lived for a while with us
so we can go to heaven
and live forever with Him.

Grow Your Faith

The incarnation—immortal Son of God taking on human flesh—is one of the most astonishing things God has ever done. What great lengths Jesus went to in order to reunite us with the Father! To what lengths will you go to reach someone who hasn't yet heeded Jesus' call?

Grow Your Child's Faith

At Christmas we celebrate the birth of Jesus, but do you know why? Jesus is unlike anyone else who ever lived; He is both God and man! Isn't it wonderful that He chose to live a human life to understand us even better? We celebrate Jesus' birth because it shows how much He loves us.

Dear Jesus, You became a person to show us Your love in a whole new way. You're so brave to leave heaven and come here because of Your love for me and everyone else. Thank You! Amen.

JESUS RADIATES THE GLORY OF GOD

We saw his true glory, the glory of the only Son of the Father. From him all the kindness and all the truth of God have come down to us.
John 1:14 CEV

The sun shines so bright
that if we looked right at it
we would hurt our eyes.

The moon reflects the sun.
It can be bright too,
but it's not too bright to look at.

God the Father
is bright like the sun.
But when Jesus became human,
we could look at Him
and see what God looks like.

Grow Your Faith

Christians are called to be Christ's body in the world. One way to think about our mission is that we reflect the glory and love of Jesus, much like the moon reflects the light of the sun. We can only reflect Jesus' glory if we spend time with Him. Are you spending so much time with Jesus that people can see Him radiating in your life?

Grow Your Child's Faith

The moon reflects the sun's light, and people can see at night. How can you reflect Jesus so others can see Him too?

Dear Jesus, thank You that You showed us what God is like. Please help me show other people what You are like. Amen.

JESUS IS THE SOURCE OF ALL BLESSINGS

*Out of his fullness we have all received grace
in place of grace already given.*
John 1:16

Grace is getting something good
you didn't work for or deserve.
Like someone taking you out for ice cream
just because they love you.

Jesus is like that.
He gives gift after gift
just because He loves us.

Grow Your Faith

Some people receive a blessing and assume it's what they deserve.
Any of us can be trapped by believing we ought to get more and
better things. It helps to count our blessings and practice seeing all
the gifts of grace that have been lavished upon us.

Grow Your Child's Faith

Are you someone who says thank you a lot? Everybody loves to be thanked and noticed for good things they've done. That includes Jesus! Make a list of what He's given you. Make it as long as you can.

Dear Jesus, You give gift after gift. Thank You! Help me be thankful to people around me. Amen!

JESUS REVEALS GOD'S GLORY

No one has ever seen God, but the one and only Son,
who is himself God and is in closest relationship
with the Father, has made him known.
John 1:18

No one can look at God.
To try would be like looking
straight at the sun.
It hurts! It's bad for us!

We cannot look at God.
But Jesus made a way
for us to see God.
In Jesus, we clearly see
how great our God is!

Grow Your Faith

When Moses came down from Mount Sinai, having received the Ten Commandments from God, his face glowed. Being in God's presence changed Moses so much that people were afraid to go near him unless he covered his face with a veil. Jesus hadn't just been in God's presence—He *is* God. Imagine how His face would have glowed, had He not "veiled" it with human flesh. Our faces may not glow, but we too are changed when we spend time in Jesus' presence.

Grow Your Child's Faith

If you get to view an eclipse, you'll be told not to look directly at the sun, even when it's blocked. If Jesus had come in all of His glory, no one could have looked at Him without going blind! *That's* the God who is inside us! How amazing!

Dear Jesus, thank You for becoming a person so we could see what God is like! Amen.

JESUS IS THE LAMB OF GOD

"Look, the Lamb of God!"
John 1:36

It used to be that God's people
apologized for their sins
by giving God a perfect lamb.

So when Jesus was called
the Lamb of God,
people should have known that pain and death
were in His future.

Grow Your Faith

The way God's people used to worship would be almost unrecognizable to us today. Animal sacrifices were simply a fact of life in ancient Israel. While we often think of lambs as baby toys or cute farm animals, in Israel they were often sacrifices. Remembering this changes what we think about what it really means for Jesus to be the Lamb of God, the final sacrifice offered for us.

Grow Your Child's Faith

Before Jesus gave Himself for us, God's people brought lambs to the temple as sacrifices given to God. Their sacrifices helped them say "I'm sorry" for what they did wrong and "Thank You" for how God forgave their sins. Why is Jesus called the Lamb of God?

Dear Jesus, You were like an innocent lamb. Thank You for loving me so much You gave Your life for mine. Amen.

JESUS CAME TO DIE FOR US

"Look, the Lamb of God, who takes away the sin of the world!"
John 1:29

How would you feel
if you knew when
and where
and how
you would die?

Would you live
trying to avoid
death?

Grow Your Faith

What must it have been like for Jesus to grow up knowing that His ministry would end with His sacrificial death? Jesus loved us so much that not even the knowledge that His death would be humiliating and painful prevented Him from teaching and healing. Jesus was faithful in carrying out the plan to save us from sin.

Grow Your Child's Faith

How far would you go to save someone you loved? Would you let yourself be hurt if it rescued someone else? That's what Jesus did! He knew we couldn't save ourselves, so He came to earth to help us. Jesus must love us very much!

Dear Jesus, You didn't have to come here to die for us, but You did it anyway. All I can do is thank You and ask You to show me how I can live for You. Amen.

13

JESUS IS OUR TEACHER

They said, "Rabbi" (which means "Teacher"),
"where are you staying?"
John 1:38

One of the main reasons Jesus came
was to show us what God is like.
He showed us by what He did,
what He said,
and how He taught.

He also taught what it means
to be a Christian—
to imitate God
and do what pleases Him.

Jesus was the master Teacher.

Grow Your Faith

Can you imagine the frustration the Pharisees and religious leaders must've felt when Jesus nimbly stepped over every logic trap they laid for Him and turned it back on them? The teachers prided themselves on their expertise in the law. But they found themselves excusing themselves from debates with an "uneducated" *carpenter*. They knew He'd best them with His knowledge of God's laws.

Grow Your Child's Faith

Imagine the best teacher you ever had, and then multiply that over and over and over again, and that's how good a teacher Jesus was. If you had been one of Jesus' students, how would you have acted anytime He started to teach?

Dear Jesus, I wish I could've heard You teach. It's so great that we can read many of Your lessons in the Bible, but I can't wait to be in heaven, where I can listen to You all the time! Amen.

14

JESUS IS THE KING OF ISRAEL

"You are the king of Israel."
John 1:49

Thrones and crowns
can be dangerous things.
Some kings will do anything
just to stay king.

King Herod did many bad things
to try to keep Jesus from being king.
But Jesus isn't *a* king—
He is *the* King of Kings.

Grow Your Faith

A king has authority over everything that happens in his kingdom. The king doesn't ask the people for permission to do what he thinks is right. With a bad king, this is very bad news. With a good king, like Jesus, this is great news! He doesn't want anyone in His kingdom to be enslaved to sin and death, so He set us all free!

Grow Your Child's Faith

What would you do if you were king or queen? One of the first things would be to make sure everyone in your kingdom was safe from enemies. And that's what King Jesus did! He fought sin and death and won. When we live in His kingdom, we obey Jesus' rules and He keeps us safe from sin and death. How can you thank King Jesus for all His work for you?

Dear Jesus, thank You for inviting us into Your kingdom! Help me to follow Your rules to show You how much I love You. Amen.

15

JESUS IS THE SON OF GOD

Then Nathanael declared, "Rabbi, you are the Son of God."
John 1:49

Jesus had a human mother,
but His Father is God.
He is both God and man.

Jesus knows His Father's personality,
He knows His Father's instructions,
and He has His Father's powers.

Grow Your Faith

The idea of Jesus as the Son of God is pretty familiar to us, but think about it afresh. Theologians have tried for years to figure out what it means for Jesus to be both God and man. Ultimately, it's a mystery! We believe it is true because the Bible says so, but how it is true is hard to comprehend. Jesus doesn't need you to understand every point of theology before you trust Him. He just needs you to believe.

Grow Your Child's Faith

Do you act like one of your parents? Do you talk like one of them? Sometimes, kids are so much like their parents that other people immediately know they are family. Jesus acted and spoke so much like the Father that some people could just tell He was the Son of God. Can people tell you are a child of God too?

Dear Jesus, thank You for showing us what God is like through Your words and actions. Help me to act like a child of God too. Amen.

16

JESUS IS THE SON OF MAN

"The Son of Man came to seek and to save the lost."
Luke 19:10

Jesus' mom was a woman named Mary.
His dad on earth was Joseph;
He had sisters and brothers and cousins.
But His Father is God in heaven.

He was a man
who was also God!

Grow Your Faith

It's really easy to talk about Jesus like He was either only God or only man. He really was both! Though we don't understand how this is possible, we know why Jesus chose to live among us: He wanted to reunite all people to God.

Grow Your Child's Faith

What do you think Jesus was like when He was your age? He had friends like you do, He studied God's Word like you do. He got sick and hungry and tired. He felt happy and sad and angry. The biggest difference is that Jesus never sinned. How can you be like Jesus this week?

Dear Jesus, thank You for being a good example of how to live the way God wants me to. Help me to be more like You. Amen.

17

JESUS SHOWS US HOW TO LOVE GOD'S HOUSE

So he took some rope and made a whip. Then he chased everyone out of the temple, together with their sheep and cattle. He turned over the tables of the moneychangers and scattered their coins.
John 2:15 CEV

How do you think
God most wants
His people to act
when they are together
worshipping Him?

Should we treat people with love and kindness
or cheat people and steal their money?

God wants us to
worship Him
and treat others well.

Grow Your Faith

If Jesus walked into your church on a typical Sunday, how do you think He'd react? Is there anything that might cause Him to make a whip and knock over the furniture? Wouldn't it be better to fix that now before Jesus shows up, angry and ready to set your church straight?

Grow Your Child's Faith

Jesus didn't show anger very often. One way to make sure He did get angry was to claim to love God but to be very mean to people. Anyone who really loves God must be good to people not bad. How can you make Jesus happy today instead of angry?

Dear Jesus, please help me to always be honest and fair. Amen.

18

JESUS IS A MIRACLE WORKER

Many people put their faith in Jesus, because they saw him work miracles.
John 2:23 CEV

When Jesus walked on the earth,
He healed the sick and blind.
He brought the dead back to life.
He walked on water
and turned a huge thunderstorm
into a puff of wind.

Jesus does miracles today too—
some we see and some we don't.

Grow Your Faith

Why is it so hard to believe that God can do anything we ask? Partially because God doesn't always do what we ask, but also partially because we think of the things we ask for as being impossible. But God can do the impossible! Jesus demonstrated this often in His ministry. What examples of Jesus' miracles give you hope that God will still do miracles today?

Grow Your Child's Faith

Jesus can do things that no one but God can do. When something we thought was impossible happens, we call it a miracle. Keep your eyes open, and you may see Jesus do a miracle!

Dear Jesus, thank You for all the work You do in the world. Please let me to see what You are doing so I can help! Amen.

19

JESUS CAME FROM HEAVEN

"No one has gone up to heaven except the Son of Man, who came down from there."
John 3:13 CEV

Jesus came down from heaven,
so we can go up to heaven.
He came to our home,
so we could live in His perfect home
forever.

Grow Your Faith

Have you ever stopped to think what Jesus gave up to come to earth? He left heaven, took on human form (including sickness, injury, and death) and exchanged worship from angels for disregard from His own creation—all so He could be falsely accused, abandoned by friends, tortured, and mocked. Wow, what a Savior!

Grow Your Child's Faith

What is the greatest example of love you have ever seen? Every act of great love is a small reflection of what Jesus did when He left His throne in heaven to come here to live with us. What's a big, loving thing you could do today?

Dear Jesus, thank You for leaving heaven to become a person and live among people. I know You loved us so much. Thank You! Amen.

20

JESUS GIVES US ETERNAL LIFE

"Whoever believes in him shall not perish but have eternal life."
John 3:16

Did you know that Jesus
is the only way
to go to heaven?

He came
to show us the way.
Our job
is to believe
in Him.

Grow Your Faith

Christians believe there is only one way to heaven. Is that what you believe? God has made it our job to offer that way to the world (2 Cor. 5:20).

Grow Your Child's Faith

It can be really scary to think about dying. But Jesus came and *broke* death so we can live forever in heaven with Him.

Dear Jesus, thank You for breaking death so we can come live with You forever in heaven! Amen.

21

JESUS IS THE LIVING WATER

"Whoever drinks the water I give will never be thirsty.
The water I give will become a spring of water gushing
up inside that person, giving eternal life."
John 4:14 NCV

When Jesus walked the earth,
people had to work hard
to have enough water
to drink and grow food
and give their animals.
So when He talked about unending water,
people listened.

Whether it comes from a faucet
or a natural fountain,
we all need water to live.
But Jesus wasn't *really* talking about water.

Grow Your Faith

In many places, a great big fountain is a symbol of well-being and prosperity. A gushing geyser of water signifies energy, joy, and plenty. If your soul is thirsty, go to the Source of the spring: Jesus.

Grow Your Child's Faith

Jesus is a gushing fountain in the middle of sand. Everybody needs water to live. For you to live forever, you need the water Jesus gives, because it's the only kind that gives you eternal life.

Dear Jesus, thank You that You are a gushing stream of living water that will never run out! Amen.

22

JESUS KNOWS EVERYTHING ABOUT US

"Come, see a man who told me everything I ever did."
John 4:29

Have you ever wanted to hide something
so you wouldn't get in trouble?
Have you ever been scared
if someone knew everything about you
that person wouldn't like you?

There's someone who knows *everything* about you
and loves you.
It's Jesus.

Grow Your Faith

It's not just children who try to hide the most "unacceptable" parts of themselves from view. The longer we've lived, the more unpresentable things there are in our pasts. We struggle to accept some of those things about ourselves. Yet we yearn for someone to know us through and through and love us nonetheless. That's Jesus.

Grow Your Child's Faith

Jesus knows everything about you, every thought you've ever had and everything you've ever done—even when you're messy and not perfect. And He *never* stops loving you.

Dear Jesus, it's a little scary that You know all my thoughts. Mostly it's wonderful though, because You know me from top to bottom, and You love me even when I mess up. Thank You! Amen.

23

JESUS IS THE SAVIOR OF THE WORLD

"We know that this man really is the Savior of the world."
John 4:42

Do you know what *Savior* means?
It means "saver," a person who saves.
If you're drowning and a lifeguard rescues you,
the lifeguard is your savior from drowning.

What do all people need
to be saved from?
What's a rescue so big
that only the Son of God
could be the Savior?

Grow Your Faith

We don't like to need to be rescued. We'd rather be the rescuers. We don't want someone to help us; we want to save ourselves. But we all need help from others. And we especially need a Savior. We need Jesus.

Grow Your Child's Faith

How do you feel when a friend sticks up for you at lunchtime? Or when your mom or dad helps you feel safe during a storm? It's a good feeling! Jesus sticks up for you and keeps you safe too. That's why He's called Savior: He can save you from anything.

Dear Jesus, thank You that You are my Savior! Amen.

24

JESUS IS TRUSTWORTHY

The man took Jesus at his word.
John 4:50

What is truth?
Something that isn't false.
Something that isn't a lie.
Something you can believe.

Jesus is truth.
Whatever He says,
you can believe.
Whatever promises He makes,
He will keep.

He promises to stay with you …
always.

Grow Your Faith

Is there something about Jesus that you believe for other people but not for yourself? Maybe you're sure that Jesus forgives this other person but you struggle to accept His forgiveness for yourself. Take what you would say to assure that other person and receive it. You can take Jesus at His word.

Grow Your Child's Faith

Who is a person in your life whose promises you believe? Jesus never lies. You can trust Him. You can believe Him. He is true.

Dear Jesus, thank You that I can trust You all the time, no matter what is happening. Would You help me trust You all the time, please? Thank You! Amen.

25

JESUS WORKS

"My Father is always working, and so am I."
John 5:17 NLT

When Jesus was on earth,
He had a job.
His Father had sent Him on a mission,
and He did it.

Now that He's in heaven,
He still works.

Grow Your Faith

The Bible tells us Jesus finished His major work and is seated at the
right hand of God (Heb. 1:3), interceding—mediating, pleading,
reconciling, interpreting—for us (Rom. 8:34). Isn't it wonderful?

Grow Your Child's Faith

Jesus never takes a vacation. Aren't you glad that when you pray, you know He hears you?

Dear Jesus, I know You're the King of the universe, but You always have time to work to help others. I love that about You. Amen.

26

JESUS IS SENT BY THE FATHER

"The Father has sent me."
John 5:36

God the Father
sent Jesus here on a mission.

He told Jesus to go to earth as a human,
show us what He is like,
bring freedom to all who are trapped,
proclaim the good news,
defeat sin and death …

and then go back to God.

Grow Your Faith

In Luke 7, Jesus encountered a Roman soldier who recognized Jesus' authority. Jesus had the authority to command illnesses and demons, but He was also under His Father's authority to carry out His mission. Jesus set aside His glory to come as a messenger, servant, and ambassador. How can you set aside your own glory to serve someone else?

Grow Your Child's Faith

When you're sent on a mission, you're automatically serving someone else. But we like to do whatever *we* want to do—especially after school! When we choose to help someone else instead, we're obeying Jesus and pleasing Him.

Dear Jesus, thank You that when Your Father sent You here, all You wanted to do was serve Him. Help me be more like You. Amen.

27

JESUS IS REVEALED BY THE SCRIPTURES

"You search the Scriptures because you think they give you eternal life. But the Scriptures point to me!"
John 5:39 NLT

Before Jesus came to earth,
God's people thought that knowing the Scriptures
would get them to heaven.
They were right—
and wrong.

They didn't need to know only
what the Scriptures talked about.
They also needed to believe in
Who the Scriptures talked about.
Jesus!

Grow Your Faith

When we read the Bible, seeing references to Jesus in the Old Testament seems simple. How could so many people have missed it? No one could have guessed what God was going to do through Jesus. It's so much greater than anyone imagined!

Grow Your Child's Faith

Have you ever looked forward to something so much you imagined every bit of it—and then, when it happened, it didn't go the way you expected? God's people had been waiting for a Savior for thousands of years, and they had a ton of ideas about what He would be like. But Jesus wasn't what they expected! To everyone who believed in Him, Jesus was even better than they had hoped.

Dear Jesus, please help me know You better by knowing Your Word. Please show me who You really are. Amen.

28

JESUS GIVES ABUNDANTLY

The disciples gathered them up and filled twelve large baskets
with what was left over from the five barley loaves.
John 6:13 CEV

Jesus fed five thousand people a full meal
from only five loaves of bread and two fish.
But notice also how much He gave.
There were twelve baskets of leftovers!

Jesus doesn't give us barely enough.
He doesn't give us just crumbs and crusts.
He gives us all we need
and even more!

Grow Your Faith

Jesus gives with a generosity that shows He is not worried about not having enough for Himself. Catch the vision! Choose to be extravagantly generous, knowing that God loves a cheerful giver (2 Cor. 9:7).

Grow Your Child's Faith

How could you be generous to someone you know? Maybe get a ton of little candies and shower them with a surprise? Or save your allowance to buy a nice present for your brother or sister? Be like Jesus and give happily.

Dear Jesus, thank You that You give us so much amazing stuff in this world and in my life! Please give me an idea of something I could give to someone I love. Amen.

29

JESUS IS THE BREAD OF LIFE

Then Jesus declared, "I am the bread of life....
Whoever eats this bread will live forever."
John 6:35, 51

Daily bread
sustains us now.
The Bread of Life
sustains us forever.

Jesus is the Bread of Life.
He doesn't just feed our bodies.
He feeds all we are.
And He does it forever.

Grow Your Faith

Jesus could have compared Himself to a rare delicacy or a food served only on special festivals. Instead He compared Himself to bread. Bread is an everyday food found in some form in cultures all around the world. By comparing Himself to bread, Jesus emphasized how He brings sustenance and strength to us in a daily and reliable—if unflashy—way.

Grow Your Child's Faith

If you could describe yourself as one kind of food, what would you be? Are you a dessert because you're so sweet, or a breakfast food because you love to wake up early to play? When Jesus described Himself, He said He was like bread. All over the world, people eat bread! Just like bread, Jesus lives in the hearts of His believers all over the world.

Dear Jesus, I know You want to live in every person so we can live with You forever. You are the Bread of Life! Amen.

JESUS TEACHES GOD'S TRUTH

"My teaching is not my own. It comes from the one who sent me."
John 7:16

If you sent someone
to give a special person an important message,
would you want your messenger
to just make up stuff to say?

No! You want the messenger
to deliver
the exact message
you sent.

Everything Jesus said and taught
was exactly what His Father
had given to Him to say.

Grow Your Faith

Jesus didn't make up stuff when He taught during His time on earth. He said only those things His Father told Him to say (John 12:49). That's how much He honored His Father and how humble He was. How do you teach God's truth?

Grow Your Child's Faith

When we're young, we trust that the adults teaching us about Jesus are telling us the truth. As we grow, we can learn for ourselves what Jesus said and did. Some people don't believe in Jesus, but you can trust your teachers who love Jesus to help you love Him too.

Dear Jesus, thank You for sending teachers to help me learn about You. Amen.

31

JESUS SHOWS US THE WAY

"Whoever follows me will never walk in darkness, but will have the light of life."
John 8:12

Some places are really, really dark.
There are caves that are totally black
because they don't let any sunlight in.
If you tried to make it through without a light,
you'd stumble and fall and get lost.

Life can be like those caves.
If we're not following Jesus' light,
we might not see what to do next.
Or we might trip on something unexpected.
And we'd definitely miss out
on some of the good things He has for us.

Grow Your Faith

Light is a powerful metaphor for Jesus. By following His example, we also live as lights in a dark world. This means we are honest and trustworthy, kind and generous. We do not speak half-truths or lies. Though we sin, we seek to eliminate that darkness in our lives by confessing those sins, bringing them into the light and repenting of them.

Grow Your Child's Faith

Are you afraid of the dark? It can be scary not to be able to see every corner of a room. Jesus lights up everywhere He goes so no darkness can be near Him. You don't have to be afraid when you walk in Jesus' light!

Dear Jesus, You are like a guide leading me through a dark cave with Your light. You stay with me all the time. You are amazing! Amen.

32

JESUS SETS US FREE

"If the Son makes you free, you will be truly free."
John 8:36 NCV

Jesus came
to set people free.
Forever!

Free from lies.
Free from fear.
Free from darkness and pain.
From evil, sin, punishment, and death.

Free to live in heaven forever.

Grow Your Faith

Jesus wanted to deliver us from every form of slavery, bondage, and captivity. His power can overcome every single obstacle in our paths. What form of bondage touches your life? How can you experience the freedom of Jesus?

Grow Your Child's Faith

Some people live like they are trapped in jail. Lots of different things can make a person feel trapped. When you are feeling trapped, Jesus can free you. Does He need to free you today?

Dear Jesus, some people don't know they can be free from sin. Please help me get Your freedom to every person who needs it! Amen.

33

JESUS IS THE LIGHT OF THE WORLD

"I am the light of the world."
John 9:5

Have you ever seen a photo
of the earth from space
showing how it's lit up
at night?

Cities show up in yellow or white.
Some places are almost black.
It is obvious
where people have lots of lights on
and where they do not.

Light is easy to see in the dark.
Jesus shines like a light
easy to see everywhere He goes.

Grow Your Faith

Spiritual darkness can be found all over the world. But there is also light. Jesus can overcome all darkness. Where in your life or the lives of those around you do you think Jesus, the Light of the World, should be shining? Will you invite Him to shine there?

Grow Your Child's Faith

Have you ever gone through a corn maze? In the daytime, it can be very easy and a lot of fun. At night, though, everything is dark. You can't see what's waiting around the corner. A friend might jump out to scare you! Wind rustling the stalks sounds spooky! The world is scary in the dark too. Walk in Jesus' light, and you'll have no reason to be afraid.

Dear Jesus, parts of this world seem dark and spooky, like something bad is there. But You bring light wherever You go. Please show me how to take You into people's lives where there is darkness. Amen.

34

JESUS IS THE GATE

"I am the gate; whoever enters through me will be saved.
They will come in and go out, and find pasture."
John 10:9

After a long trip or a long day at school,
seeing the door to your home
might be the best
thing in the world.

Inside that door are all the comforts
of the place where you're most relaxed.
When you close that door,
it keeps you safe and sheltered.

Jesus is like a door
we pass through
to get to comfort and protection from harm.

Grow Your Faith

A door is both a barrier and portal. It stands between you and the
night, and it is the way into warmth and peace. Similarly, the gate
to the sheepfold keeps the sheep in and the wolves out. Is there
a door you need to open to someone today or a gate you need to
shut?

Grow Your Child's Faith

Jesus is like a gate that closes against wolves, protecting the sheep, and opens when it's time for the sheep to eat. That doesn't mean life is perfect, though. Sometimes, bad things still happen to the sheep. The most important way that Jesus is a gate is when we think about heaven. He's the only way in!

Dear Jesus, I want all the people I care about to come through You and go to heaven. Please help me show them how to get to You! Amen.

35

JESUS FILLS LIFE TO THE FULLEST

"I came so that everyone would have life, and have it in its fullest."
John 10:10 CEV

Some people can make following Jesus
seem boring and full of rules.
They love to talk about what they don't do
and what they shouldn't do
and what they'd *never* do.

Jesus said He came
so people could love their lives.
Jesus gives us peace and joy
the world can't understand.

Grow Your Faith

Until we reach the point where we can truly accept our secure position in Christ, we'll never stop trying to *establish* our position in Christ. That useless effort brings with it comparing ourselves to others and trying to prove our worth. It brings only misery, never the lasting peace and joy Jesus intended. When we accept Christ's utter acceptance, the abundant life He promised is suddenly our whole experience.

Grow Your Child's Faith

Life is sometimes fun and sometimes boring. Sometimes it's easy, and sometimes it's really hard or painful. But when we love Jesus, we can always run into His arms. When we remember His love for us, we can handle going back out where things can be hard.

Dear Jesus, thank You for being with me, especially when things get hard. Help me remember that You are in charge, no matter what! Amen.

36

JESUS IS THE GOOD SHEPHERD

*"I am the good shepherd. The good shepherd
gives his life for the sheep."*
John 10:11 NCV

A shepherd isn't just a sheep babysitter.
He is also like a secret agent
whose job is to take care of sheep.

If lions, wolves, or sheep-stealers comes,
a good shepherd—a really good shepherd—
will fight to the death to protect the sheep.

Do you see now what Jesus meant
when He said He is the Good Shepherd?

Grow Your Faith

List the people you would die to protect. The love you feel for them is the same love Jesus feels for all of us. How did that love translate to action in Jesus' ministry? How can that love translate to action in your own life?

Grow Your Child's Faith

Jesus calls Himself a shepherd, and He calls us His sheep. Sometimes we feel like sheep, wandering around, wondering where to go, where our food and drink are going to come from, if someone will keep us safe. Jesus isn't just a good shepherd; He's the best possible Shepherd.

Dear Jesus, thank You for leading me and taking care of my needs. Thank You even more for protecting me so well that I don't even need to worry if I am safe. Amen.

37

JESUS IS THE RESURRECTION AND THE LIFE

"I am the resurrection and the life. The one who believes in me will live, even though they die; and whoever lives by believing in me will never die."
John 11:25–26

For everyone who loves Jesus,
death is not the end
but a new beginning
that has no end.

Grow Your Faith

The entire Christian faith hinges on Jesus' resurrection. Without it, our faith would be in vain, and we would still be stuck in sin and doomed to hell (1 Cor. 15:17). Jesus died once to conquer death forever. He rose from the dead so His followers can live with Him forever.

Grow Your Child's Faith

Jesus lived a perfect life. Some people didn't like Him, and they killed Him. But Jesus beat death and came back to life! Because Jesus beat death, we can beat death too. We just have to trust Jesus to give us new life with Him.

Dear Jesus, thank You for giving us so much to celebrate. Thank You for new life! I'm so excited to live with You in heaven. Amen.

38

JESUS IS COMPASSIONATE

Jesus cried.
John 11:35 NCV

We see Jesus teaching
or healing people
or walking on the water
or in pain on the cross.

And sometimes Jesus was sad.
And then He would cry.

Grow Your Faith

Why did Jesus cry at Lazarus's grave? Some Bible teachers say Jesus was moved to tears because others were crying, or maybe because His friend Lazarus had died. But maybe He cried because death separated loved ones from each other and from God. Maybe, in that moment when everyone was wailing, He saw the whole reason He had come to earth.

Grow Your Child's Faith

Has anyone you loved died? It hurts so bad, doesn't it? It can help to remember that Jesus knew what it felt like to lose someone He loved. His own dear friend Lazarus died. It helps to know that Jesus hurts too when we hurt, because He knows how it feels.

Dear Jesus, I'm glad You know how I feel when I'm sad. Amen.

39

JESUS IS A HUMBLE SERVANT

He put some water into a large bowl. Then
he began washing his disciples' feet.
John 13:5 CEV

Can you imagine a president
on his knees rubbing the feet
of the dirtiest homeless person?

Can you imagine a queen
getting her gown filthy
to pull an orphan out of the mud?

What about the Son of God
giving the servants the night off
and handwashing His followers' dirty feet?

Grow Your Faith

Christ could be a servant because He understood that power in
God's kingdom isn't like power in the world. Servants are leaders
in God's kingdom. Those of us who haven't learned that yet act
like the disciples and jockey for the best position (Luke 9:46).
When we finally learn what real leadership looks like, we can
imitate Jesus. That's when true humility and servanthood become
open to us.

Grow Your Child's Faith

Even though Jesus is the King of the universe and the Son of God, He showed us it is more important to serve others than to be served. What's the most generous or helpful thing you can think of to do for someone in your family today? Do it!

Dear Jesus, help me know that You love me so much that I can serve others like You did! Amen.

40

JESUS IS OUR EXAMPLE

"I have given you an example to follow. Do as I have done to you."
John 13:15 NLT

Some people expect you
to do what they say
and not what they do.

But we copy what people do
not what they say.
We only do what they say
if *they* do what they say.

If you want to know
how to love Jesus well,
copy Him!

Grow Your Faith

The next time you find yourself lecturing your children to do something you don't do yourself, consider saving your breath. Work instead on demonstrating what you want your children to do. Make it a good habit for yourself. Then you will demonstrate how important it is to you that your children do it too. Jesus demonstrated everything He asked us to do; we should strive to do the same.

Grow Your Child's Faith

Every last thing Jesus wants us to do, He showed us how to do. Jesus came and lived a perfect life to show us the best way for His followers to live. Can you be a role model to your friends and show them Jesus?

Dear Jesus, I'm so glad You came and lived out all the examples I would need so I can live the life You want me to have and treat others the way You want me to treat them. Amen.

41

JESUS GIVES US A HOME IN HEAVEN

"I am going there to prepare a place for you."
John 14:2 NCV

The night before Jesus died,
He told His friends
He was going to leave them.

This scared them so much!
But Jesus said He was going away
for a reason.

He said He was leaving them
so He could get a place ready
where they could go and be with Him.

Grow Your Faith

The first question two of Jesus' disciples asked Him was, "Where are you staying?" (John 1:38). He answered, "You will see" (v. 39). They saw He didn't have a permanent home but constantly moved around (Luke 9:58). Now they wondered something similar: Where was Jesus going, and why couldn't they go with Him? "I'll go get it ready," Jesus said, "and when everything is set, you can come and see." No matter how unsettled your life feels, rest in Jesus' promise that He will welcome you home.

Grow Your Child's Faith

When you're going to throw a special party for someone, you have a lot of work to do first. You have to get the room ready, invite the guests, make special treats, and buy presents. Then, when everything is ready, your guests come and have the best time. That's what Jesus is doing right now: preparing a party for us, a party we will never have to leave! How can you get ready to meet Jesus face-to-face?

Dear Jesus, I can't wait for You to come get us. You've been preparing this party for a long time—it's going to be amazing! Amen.

42

JESUS IS THE WAY, THE TRUTH, AND THE LIFE

Jesus answered, "I am the way and the truth and the life."
John 14:6

If you had to pick three words
to describe yourself,
which three would you pick?

Jesus' three are:
way,
truth, and
life.

The way to where? To God and heaven.
The truth about what? He *is* truth.
What life? Eternal life.

Grow Your Faith

People around the world hold many different beliefs about how to arrive in heaven or if heaven even exists. Although some believe that there are many possible paths to heaven, Jesus revealed that there is only one. Only through Him can we find the path to live eternally in heaven. This is the truth.

Grow Your Child's Faith

Some people don't believe Jesus is the Son of God. Some believe there is no real truth. And some people believe the Christian life is dumb. That's why Jesus left us with such an important job when He went back to heaven—He told us to tell everyone about Him so they would know the way, the truth, and the life too! Who can you share Jesus with this week?

Dear Jesus, You are the way, the truth, and the life. Help me shine Your light so others can find their way to You! Amen.

43

JESUS IS OUR PEACE

"Peace I leave with you; my peace I give you."
John 14:27

Sometimes we think
peace just means no war.

But peace isn't just
when something is not there.
Peace comes when something—or Someone—is.

Grow Your Faith

It's possible to be floating quietly in a pristine pool in a luxurious destination and still be full of anxiety. It's also possible to be surrounded by chaos and still be in a state of tranquility. No matter your circumstances, ask Jesus to provide you with perfect peace today.

Grow Your Child's Faith

Jesus had a different kind of peace from what humans can get on their own. Just like He is light and life, He also is peace. It's what comes to you when you are 100 percent resting in Jesus.

Dear Jesus, many times I don't feel any peace at all, especially not Your kind of special peace. But I want it. Teach me what it means to rest in You. I want to just sit back and invite Your peace to flow all through me. Amen.

44

JESUS IS THE TRUE VINE

"I am the true vine."
John 15:1

What happens to a branch
that falls off its tree?
What happens to a flower
that is picked from its stem?

A plant starts to die
as soon as it's separated from its roots.
We only grow strong and fruitful
as we stay connected to Jesus.

Grow Your Faith

One of the easiest ways to know we are living in Christ is that we grow, thrive, and bear fruit. When we are becoming more like Jesus, we know we are connected to Him! What habit could you develop or continue that "plugs" you into Jesus?

Grow Your Child's Faith

Fruit grows when a fruit tree, bush, or vine is getting everything it needs to be healthy. If you pick fruit from a branch, the branch will grow more fruit. But the branch won't grow anything—and will actually die—if you cut it off from its plant. That's a picture of how we grow in Jesus. We are like branches that have to stay attached to Jesus to be healthy and become what He wants us to be. We stay attached by loving Him, reading the Bible, going to church, and letting Him be free to do anything He wants in our hearts.

Dear Jesus, I love being a branch of You and seeing what fruit You grow in me! Amen.

45

JESUS COMMANDS US TO LOVE ONE ANOTHER

"My command is this: Love each other as I have loved you."
John 15:12

When Jesus told us
to love each other
as He loved us,
what did He mean?

Did He mean to love
as much as He loved us?
Or maybe to love
in the way He loved us?

What if it's both?

Grow Your Faith

How would you characterize Jesus' love for His followers? Certainly it was selfless, generous, freely given, forgiving, and sacrificial. His love also called His disciples to action, service, and even correction. He brought them to places of safety, reflection, instruction, and provision. In short, He loves in the way a good parent loves. And we are to love each other in the same way. How can you do that today?

Grow Your Child's Faith

What's your favorite story about Jesus loving someone? How could you copy Jesus and love someone else the way He loved?

Dear Jesus, You are love. It's who You are and what You're made of. Because You love me so much, I want to love others in the same ways. Please teach me how to love as You love! Amen.

46

JESUS AND GOD SHARE EVERYTHING

"Everything that the Father has is mine."
John 16:15 CEV

Jesus and His Father share everything.
The Father doesn't keep
anything from His Son.
What does that include?

Grow Your Faith

Sometimes we have trouble believing Jesus will be generous giving us everything that we need. What should we do or think when the Lord doesn't intervene with provision or power or healing or influence, even though we know He could? Maintaining our solid faith in His care for us even when He doesn't "come through" as we wanted Him to is one of the hardest challenges of Christianity. What helps you rejoice in those times? Read Habakkuk 3:17–18 and see if you agree with the prophet's words.

Grow Your Child's Faith

It's nice to know that Jesus shares everything with His Father, isn't it? Together the God the Father, Jesus, and the Holy Spirit created everything. Because Jesus created everything and shares it with the Father, He cares how everything is treated. Be good to plants and animals, and especially be loving to other people.

Dear Jesus, You own everything, but You're not stingy or selfish about it. You give and give like Your treasures will never run out—because they won't! Amen.

47

JESUS PRAYS FOR US

"I pray for them."
John 17:9

The next time you're feeling
like nobody cares about you,
just remember that you
are on Jesus' prayer list!

Isn't it incredible to think
that Jesus has you in mind
when He sits down
to talk to His Father?

Grow Your Faith

It's amazing that the One who envisioned, created, and maintains the whole universe with all those moving parts has every person on His heart in a single-minded, intense way. Is there someone in your life who you could lavish your attention upon this week?

Grow Your Child's Faith

Jesus prays for us, and He also asks us to love others like He loves us. One way we can do that is to pray for others too. Make a list of five people you want to pray for. Pick one or two things you want to talk about with Jesus for each person. Say a prayer for all five people every night for a week.

Dear Jesus, I know You don't automatically say yes to everything I pray for. I know that some of my prayers aren't what You're planning. But some of them are. Please teach me how prayer works. Amen.

48

JESUS IS KING OF KINGS

"My kingdom is not of this world.... My kingdom is from another place."
John 18:36

Jesus is King of all the earth.
But not many people
let Him be King of them here.

That didn't bother Jesus when He was on earth.
He came to teach, heal, love, and die.
He knew this world would be His kingdom,
but something big had to happen first.

Grow Your Faith

An American embassy in another country is considered part of America, just like a French embassy outside of France is a part of France, and so on. Similarly, a king's kingdom is wherever he is honored as sovereign. How are you honoring Jesus as the King of your heart and life?

Grow Your Child's Faith

Jesus is King, but many people live in rebellion against Him. Christians know that Jesus is King and tell others about Him. When someone comes to faith and hails Him as King, it makes Jesus so happy. And He will remember those who serve Him.

Dear Jesus, You are my King! Teach me to hear and understand Your commands so I do the work of Your kingdom. Amen.

49

JESUS WAS THE SUFFERING SAVIOR

Pilate ordered that Jesus be taken away and whipped. The soldiers made a crown from some thorny branches … and hit him in the face.

John 19:1–3 NCV

Jesus knows the world
is broken by sin.
And He knew His life
would be full of pain
because of other people's sins.

But all of that pain,
and even death,
could not keep Jesus
from coming to earth
to save us.

Grow Your Faith

Jesus knew there would be torture and abuse before the cross. Every Jew in Jerusalem had seen how the Romans treated criminals condemned to crucifixion. Jesus not only submitted Himself to wrongful arrest, false accusation, and death for crimes He didn't commit; Jesus also endured additional assaults and maltreatment at the hands of the soldiers and crowd. Read and reflect upon Hebrews 12:1–3. How do these verses inspire you?

Grow Your Child's Faith

Have you ever been bullied? It doesn't always matter how nice you are. Some people will treat you badly anyway. Jesus faced the worst kinds of meanness. He wasn't bullied; He was killed. Jesus died loving the people who hurt Him, and He loves you too.

Dear Jesus, I almost can't bear to think of how You were treated on that day. You loved those people, and look what they did! I'm so glad Your pain is over. Amen.

50

JESUS DIED ON THE CROSS

Jesus was nailed to the cross.
John 19:18 CEV

When the Romans really wanted
to punish a criminal,
they would nail him to a cross.

He wouldn't die quickly on a cross.
He would suffer a long time first.

Grow Your Faith

Have you ever psyched yourself up to do something hard—and possibly humiliating—and then, when the moment came, you backed out? We can all understand what it's like to question our earlier commitments. Even Jesus wept and thought about calling for a rescue. But He went through with His sacrifice. What a Savior! What does Jesus' faithful example inspire you to do?

Grow Your Child's Faith

Would you ever take someone else's punishment? Would you ever let people say mean and untrue things about you and *then* take someone else's punishment? What if they hurt you and called you terrible names? That's what Jesus did for us on the cross. How can you thank Him for being so kind to you?

Dear Jesus, no one could do what You did for us. Thank You for Your amazing love. You are awesome, and all I can do is love You. Amen.

51

JESUS TOOK OUR PLACE AND OUR PUNISHMENT

For God made Christ, who never sinned, to be the offering for our
sin, so that we could be made right with God through Christ.
2 Corinthians 5:21 NLT

Do you know why Jesus
died for us?

Remember the innocent lamb
the priests would offer
to pay the punishment
for a person's sin?

People kept doing wrong things,
as all people—even you and I—will do.
So priests kept offering lambs
over and over and over again.

Jesus the Lamb died
so you and I could live.
He was our offering.
He gave up His life to save us.

Grow Your Faith

Jesus' death did what a lamb's death never could. He secured forgiveness for everyone who believes in Him. Jesus paid it all one time because of His great love for us.

Grow Your Child's Faith

Have you ever been punished for something you didn't do? It's not fair when that happens. You probably wouldn't choose to be grounded when you hadn't done anything wrong. Jesus is different. He chose to be punished so we wouldn't be.

Dear Jesus, only You could've done what had to be done to save us. Please help me live saying thank You for what You did for me. Amen.

52

JESUS IS RISEN!

"I have seen the Lord!"
John 20:18

After He died on a cross,
Jesus came back to life on the third day.
After two days of thinking they'd been wrong,
Jesus' friends saw Him alive!

What do you think they felt on Saturday?
And then what was it like for them on Sunday?
Jesus came back from the dead!
Our Savior lives!

Grow Your Faith

Jesus came to do many things. He came to show what the invisible God is like. He came to set the captives free. He came to do His Father's will. He came to fulfill Scripture and set up a new kingdom. He came to seek and save that which was lost. He came to solve the problem of sin, pay the punishment for humankind, reconcile God and us, and usher in the Devil's defeat. He came to break death. The resurrection is the linchpin of history. Without it, as 1 Corinthians 15:12–19 tells us, our faith would be worthless, and we would all spend eternity separated from God.

Grow Your Child's Faith

If Jesus hadn't beaten death by coming back to life, He wouldn't have the power to break the power of death over you and me so we can go to heaven. But Jesus *did* destroy death's power! We will live with Him forever!

Dear Jesus, You are the greatest warrior ever! You defeated sin, which held us prisoner. And You let death take You down, so You could defeat it three days later! Thank You for dying for me on the cross, but mostly for coming back from the dead so I can live with You forever! Amen.

Devotions to Grow the Whole Family's Faith

Family devotions don't have to be dull! Breathe fresh life into this special time with the David C Cook Family Devotions. By bringing delight to doctrine through a poetic style and engaging illustrations, each devotion graciously points you to Scripture to grow your family's faith as well as your own.

Available in print and digital wherever books are sold